Lawyers!
Lawyers!
Lawyers!

Lawyers! Lawyers! Lawyers!

A Cartoon Collection
Edited by S. Gross

CB

CONTEMPORARY
BOOKS
CHICAGO

Library of Congress Cataloging-in-Publication Data

Lawyers! lawyers! lawyers! : a cartoon collection / edited by S.
    Gross.
            p.   cm.
        ISBN 0-8092-3722-9 (cloth)
            1. Lawyers—United States—Caricatures and cartoons.
        2. American wit and humor, Pictorial.   I. Gross, S. (Sam)
        NC1426.L38   1994
        741.5'973—dc20   93-45963
                                                                        CIP

Published by Contemporary Books, Inc.
Two Prudential Plaza, Chicago, Illinois 60601-6790
Manufactured in the United States of America
International Standard Book Number: 0-8092-3722-9
10   9   8   7   6   5   4   3   2   1

To Mick Stevens,
who handed me a subpoena.
I ran with it.

Acknowledgments

Cartoons copyrighted by *The New Yorker* are indicated throughout the book.

Some of the cartoons in this collection have appeared in the following books and periodicals and are reprinted by permission of the artists: *Case and Comment, Golf, Golf, Golf, Insurance Review, The Lawyer's Joke Book, National Lampoon, National Law Journal, Official Detective Group, Philadelphia Inquirer,* and *Saturday Review.*

Lawyers! Lawyers! Lawyers!

"I can see what's causing the problem—
you've got a lawyer on your back."

1

STOP AND SUE
THE ROSES.

"At best, I could probably get you an acquittal in a mock trial."

© 1989 The New Yorker Magazine, Inc.

"How very exciting!
I have never before met a Second *Amendment lawyer!"*

"I find the defendant guilty."

*"Would everyone check to see they have an attorney?
I seem to have ended up with two."*

"It's your babysitter's lawyer."

"Miss Benson, I wish you'd stop saying
'What will they think of next?'"

9

"How much longer do we have to wait out this
Chapter Eleven of yours?"

"It's finally over—Frank's lawyer got the apartment, and my lawyer got our two cars and the beach house."

"Am I still entitled to just one phone call if I have my own phone?"

13

"We're moving the legal library into your office, since you have most of the books."

"My lawyer, the one who negotiated the bonus
of $1,500,000 if I bat over .212 for the season,
says to pitch him high and inside!"

15

"I am Don Hernando, immigration lawyer."

"Read me that part about animal rights again!"

*"Objection sustained.
Erase that last statement from the videotape."*

*"Oh, dear, when we fired Hooper from the law firm,
I never expected to see him again."*

"Ask the judge if we may borrow the murder weapon."

"I'm a partner trapped in an associate's body."

"I thought the Supreme Court outlawed that!"

"I have to hang up now, Mom. I think I have my first client."

© 1990 The New Yorker Magazine, Inc.

25

"Ed's a lawyer slash actor, Ron's a lawyer slash filmmaker,
and Beverly's a lawyer slash playwright."

27

*"Let us see some dramatic poses in your summation.
Daumier is in the courtroom!"*

BASIC INSTINCTS OF MAN

LITIGATE | SETTLE

Kinnstein

ANDROCLES AND THE LAWYER

*"Thanks bunches. By the way,
are you licensed to practice in this state?"*

CAUTION: I BRAKE FOR ANIMALS AND HAVE A GOOD LAWYER

THE PRIMAL
LOOPHOLE
FROM WHICH
AN ENTIRE
PROFESSION
EXPLODED

E. SUBITZKY

"Don't tell me—another day of pro bono!"

"Not another change of venue, Counselor!"

"Help! Help! My son, the lawyer, is drowning!"

© 1989 The New Yorker Magazine, Inc.

"Do you know Kimberly, my attorney?"

"Young lady, I'm married to him!
What do you mean I can't get in to see him?"

38

*"Darling, the entire firm of Howlston, Martin, Webb,
Penner & Connolly are trying to save our marriage.
Are we going to let them down?"*

39

"He wants a lawyer. . . . Which cell do we keep the lawyers in?"

"That one's not for sale. It's my ex-wife's lawyer."

"I'm a lawyer, damn it, and there's
nothing wrong with being a lawyer, right?"

Legal Notices

NOTICE OF INTENT

I, Shirley Janison, will dispose of this box of baseball cards which has been cluttering up the hall closet since 1966 on May 9, 1992.

NOTICE TO CREDITOR

Notice is hereby given to Will J. from Howard T. that you will never see a _cent_ of that ten dollars you claim to have won from me in last week's Scrabble game, because "quixoty" is _not_, and will _never be_, a word.

NOTICE OF LEGAL PERMISSION TO DO SOMETHING HORRENDOUS

Pursuant to the authority of the Board of Directors of the Acme Corporation, notice is hereby served to the residents of Woodland Farms that a nuclear power plant will be built right next to your swimming pool.

NOTICE OF IRRESPONSIBILITY

To all patrons of Sheila's Hair Shack: If you don't like your new haircuts, you can lump 'em.

R. Chv

LAWYER
STATESMAN

(NEVER TOOK
THE FIFTH)

"Whose idea was it to use an arbitrator, anyway?"

"Would you carry a Lawyer-Client/Client-Lawyer Dictionary?"

"Last week I'm running an electronics plant in Ohio—today I'm a holy man in Kashmir. What won't my tax lawyer think of next?"

"Bless me, Father, for I have applied to law school. . . ."

"Today my client turned and hugged me."

"Penny and I share everything except the same attorney."

"Now, everything that is irrelevant must be in alphabetical order."

The Alleged Perpetrators
BRONX

52

"May I ask you, Miss Howre,
what made you select a homeopathic attorney?"

"He said he always wanted to do this at four in the morning
with an initial stock offering, and then he said
he was going off to Tahiti to paint."

"Thank you, sir, and here's my card."

". . . and then it hit me. I've reached that stage in life where most of my friends are lawyers."

56

"In case you're wondering, it'll hold up in court."

JUDGES

SOFT   HANGING   CIRCUIT

59

*"As long as I'm teaching you about sex and reproduction,
it might also be highly appropriate to give you some
instruction on prenuptial agreements."*

"Say—hold on a minute."

"Ladies and gentlemen, and guests of the jury. . . ."

"There's one thing about the law I always wanted to know but was afraid to ask: Where in the hell do all the lawyer jokes come from?"

"What's a tort?"

WYNSOM
LEWSOM
ATTORNEYS AT LAW

Bernard Schoenbaum

"Stop making such a case of it!
A lot of young lawyers kick their fathers out of their law firms!"

PAWN   KNIGHT   BISHOP   ROOK   ATTORNEY   QUEEN   KING

"Let's find a voir dire *in progress and scare the living hell out of them."*

"You'd better show me the proper respect, sonny!
I kissed a lot of ass to get this job!"

*"Life is too cruel! To witness such an open-and-shut case
just when I've been disbarred!"*

LETTER OF
THE LAW

SPIRIT OF
THE LAW

A. BACALL

"If you want my advice, any man who represents himself, or engages me to represent him, has a fool for a lawyer."

76

*"Counsel will kindly refrain from testifiduction and hippothanatology—
in lay terms, leading the witness and beating a dead horse."*

77

" 'Season's Greetings' looks OK to me.
Let's run it by the legal department."

THE DEFENSE NEVER RESTS

"Well, there was a Malone who tried that in 1942 and won, but, on the other hand, there was a Parker who tried it in '63 and lost."

" . . . It was a dark and stormy afternoon. My client glared at me
as he realized I wasn't taking notes about his murder trial
but was, in fact, writing this novel. . . ."

I just want to inject a word of caution into these proceedings: If we adopt laws, we're sure to get lawyers.''

"Hi, I'm Larry, and I'll be your process server."

" 'Mea culpa'? What the hell kind of an answer is that?"

J. WHITLOCK
AND
PARDNERS

LAW FIRM

*"The merger is on Tuesday, the ninth. Are you sure all the papers
are in order? That it was properly proofread? Remember,
you're an associate coming up for a partnership."*

"The doctor is in court on Tuesdays and Wednesdays."

"Of course it's down. Even computers hate doing legal research."

So what you're saying, Dad, is that when a person has a problem, they call a lawyer like you to fix it. If you fix it, you get a lot of money, but if you don't fix it, you also get a lot of money?
SIPRESS

"Up until now I never thought of this as copyright infringement."

"For God's sake, Mildred. You're a lawyer, not a lawyerette!"

TINY CLAIMS COURT

Neighbor's dog chewed pencil.

Flapjack mix from Dalemart bought by N.M. was spoiled.

E·Z BATTER
FLAPJACKS
A

While sewing at T.F.'s house, claimant pricked self with borrowed needle.

R. Chast

DECISIONS, DECISIONS, DECISIONS

93

"I now pronounce your relationship litigatable."

"The lawyers took everything."

"I understand he's under house arrest."

"Lights, camera—bequeath!"

Index of Artists